Lowry's Places

Lowry's early years as an artist were framed on the one hand by the suffocating dramas of late Victorian art and on the other, the airy horizons opened up by French Impressionism. Impressionism was essentially an art of landscape but as Lowry gravitated towards the industrial scene in the hope that he could make his mark because nobody else had tackled it, he found Impressionism's flickering brush strokes and broken colour inappropriate for his vision. Although a Whistler, or more pertinently Lowry's teacher Valette, had applied Impressionism to the murk of the nineteenth century cityscape, this atmospheric approach did not satisfy Lowry. Picture making in the modern era stressed the flatness of the picture plane before the illusion … But Lowry found this moc… notion not via theory but b… absorption of what the flat Manchester plain presented him and the expanse of ofte… monochrome grey white sky above it. With these as a given, his vision evolved.

As this exhibition traces, we are looking at a vision rather than a depiction and the quintessential place - above all other Lowry places - is his painting room, where works were shuffled from easel to floor and back again and where notes he had made on the streets formed and reformed in picture after picture. Lowry's Places all came from that one place - his imagination as realised in his painting room.

… lenders, … private, to this … and in particular to the invaluable support of Carol Ann Lowry. The exhibition has been curated by Lindsay Brooks and Merlin James has helped us open up some fresh perspectives on Lowry's sense of place and where we, in turn, place Lowry.

David Alston, Galleries Director

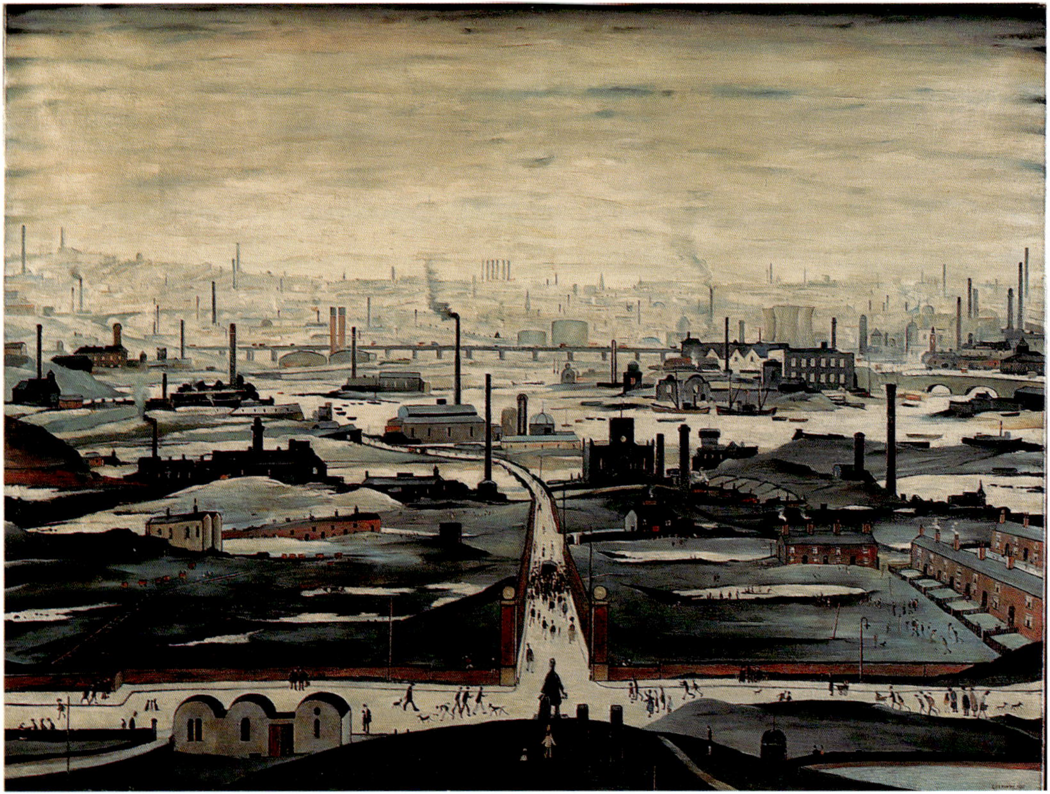

Lowry's Places: the exhibition

Lindsay Brooks

Lowry's Places is about the type of choice Lowry made: sweeping views of the industrial north, panoramas of countryside and coastline, and close-up views of corners and blind frontages. Lowry is identified with cities in the popular imagination and his strange and solid seascapes and bleak landscapes are less well-known. The exhibition illustrates this rarely acknowledged strand in his work that is a counterpoint to grander, more familiar industrial scenes.

In these, Lowry used certain churches, viaducts and factories as 'building blocks'. The underlying rhythm of many pictures was drawn from known locations and the results were places that seem half-familiar but which were imaginative inventions. Sometimes he adopted a high vantage point such as in *Industrial Landscape,* 1953, opposite. The scene unfolds in a framework of locked grids, pulled together with spots of red. In the distance, Lowry has crammed a large number of factories, cooling towers, chimneys and warehouses, stretching to the horizon and melded them all in a creamy haze of sky.

In contrast, the landscapes in and around Cumbria, for example *A Landmark*, 1936 (postcard 4) or *The Lake*, 1951 (postcard 6), seem to be slotted together out of flat sections that have a suspended, floating quality. The paintings provide an illusion of depth, but it is a theatrical depth made out of flats. The viewer is made aware that spaces cannot be filled. Instead, there is nothing but the flats and the tantalising spaces of unknown depth that lie between them. The small amount of modelling and colour contrasts only accentuates the fact that it is impossible to judge distances. The hills are so minimal that it seems impossible for anyone to enter these spaces. There is no air, no sympathetic and inviting perspective and scarcely any convincing light. These pictures represent a topsy-turvy view of landscape, somewhere uninhabitable.

When Lowry painted 'beauty spots' such as the Lake District, he

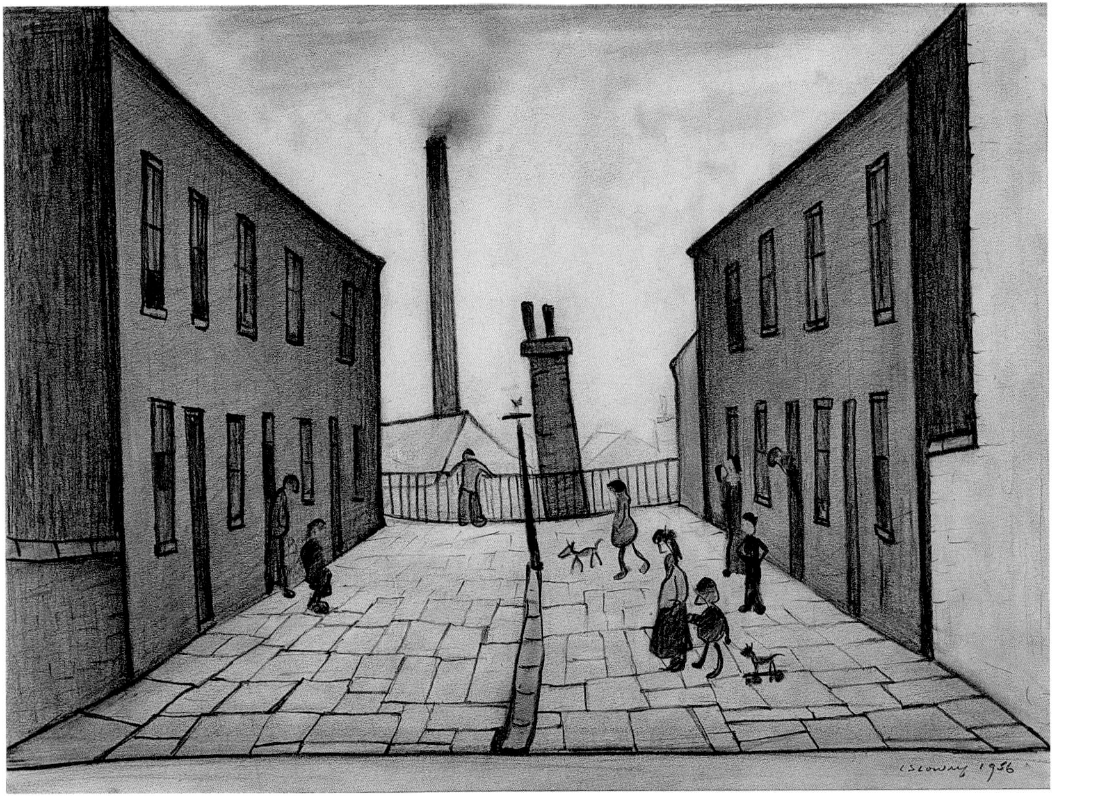
LSLowry 1956

turned upside down the usual idea of the place as picturesque. He fashioned his own version of an uncomfortable, lonely landscape. This version of British landscape was not the sole measure of the place: some views of the countryside of the 1920s (included in the exhibition) are optimistic and pastoral. But a sense of the country as desolate was, for most of the time and in the end, the dominant point of view (postcards 4, 5 & 6).

It should be a relief to turn to the drawings of city streets and these are given special attention in the exhibition. Lowry sketched corners, doorways and strange buildings which caught his eye. Blank facades, flights of steps and narrow streets vanish somewhere indecipherable (*Francis Terrace*, 1956, opposite; *Steps* c 1940, page 14) and these motifs recur, creating space that is uninviting. There, in those corners or under the towering blocks, the walls press in and movement is stifled. Figures sometimes stand stock still and even those walking seem to have at least one foot rooted to the spot. No one is going anywhere, and there is nowhere much to go.

Lowry's precise vision may not be our own, but it is a familiar point of view. The alienating city is a common, shared and contemporary experience. As viewers, we have plenty of opportunity to be diverted away from Lowry and his version of Britain as an unrelentingly oppressive space. No doubt we take our chances and enjoy our traditional scenery in the usual, pleasurable ways. On the other hand, it is invigorating to stand at the edge and look over. Equally, it is hard to resist Lowry's unremitting stare. It is especially pleasurable to look at a painting and have it glare at you.

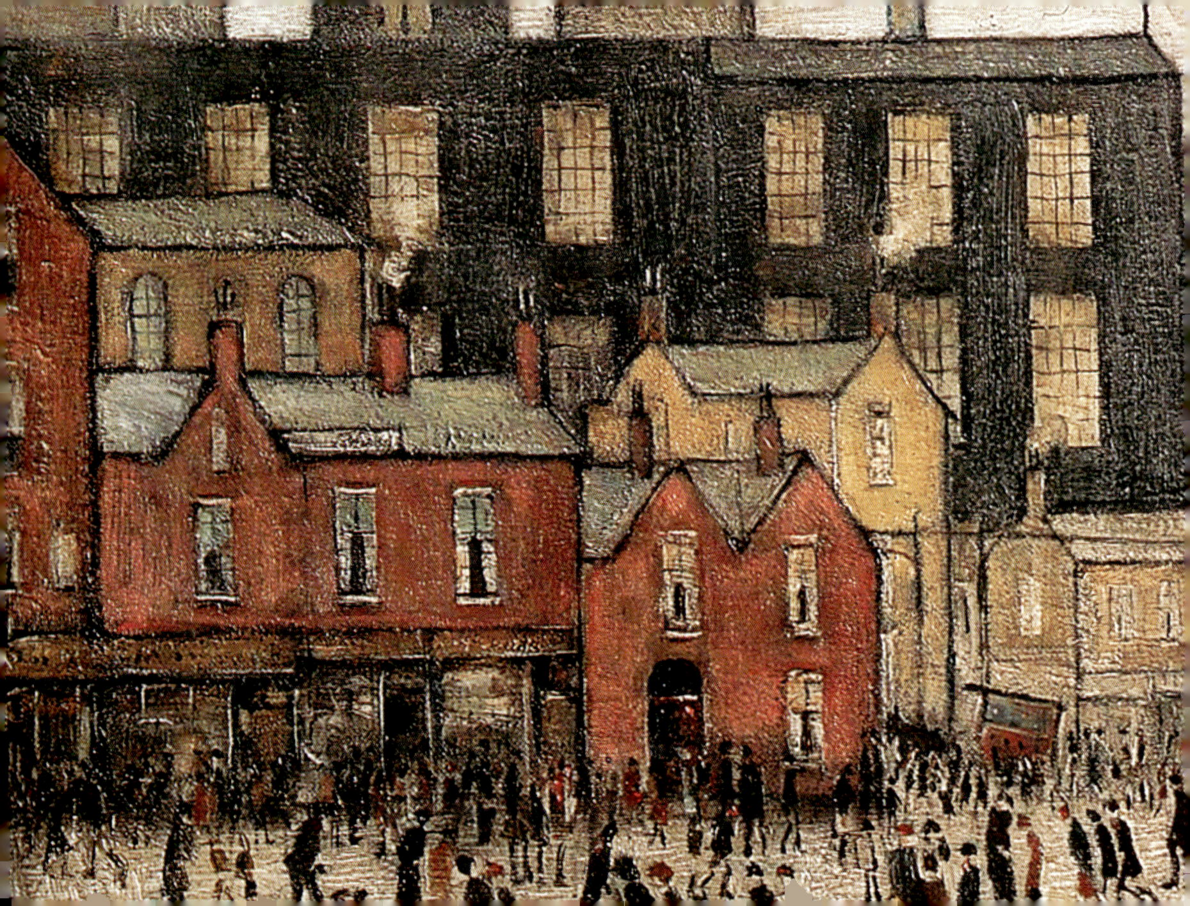

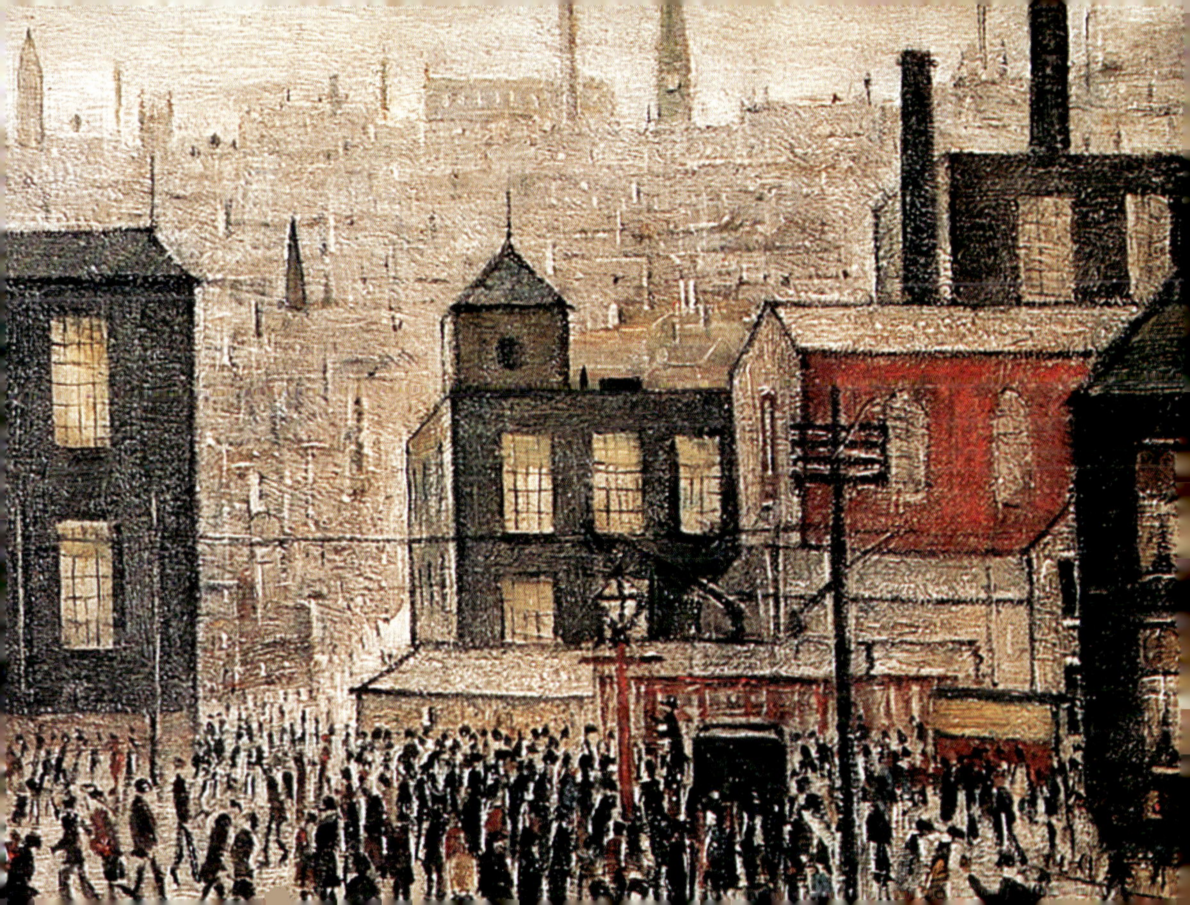

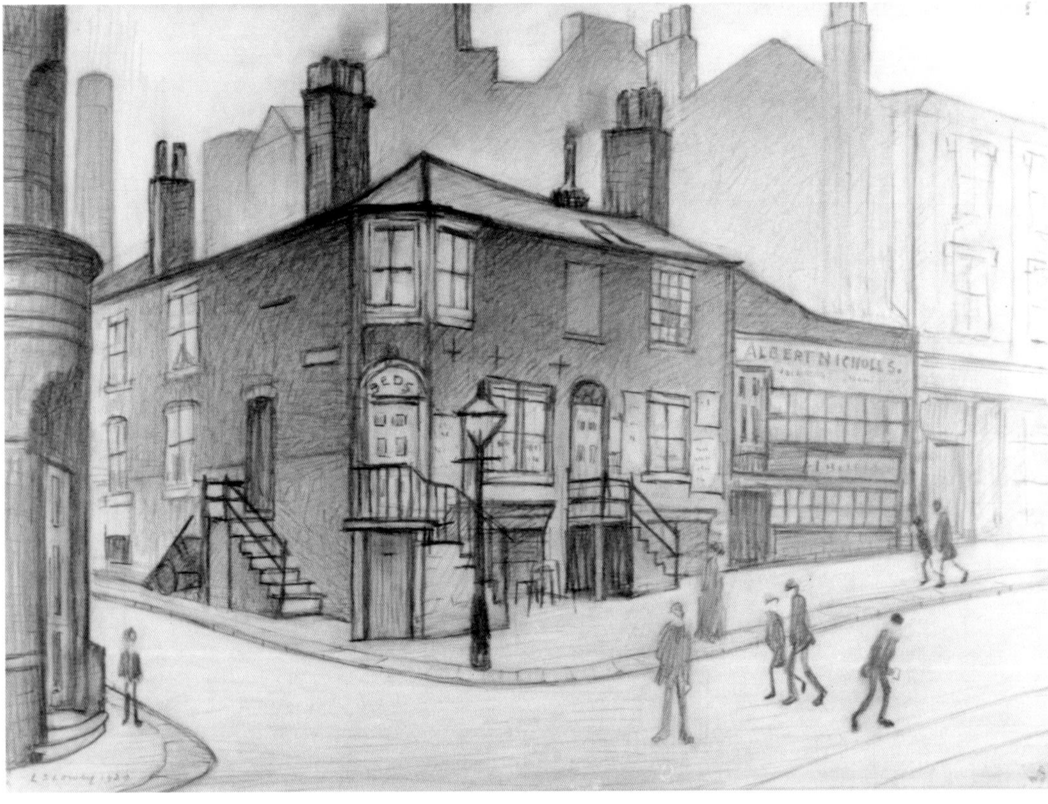
BEDS
ALBERT NICHOLLS

Lowry's World Picture

Merlin James

L. S. Lowry is often thought of as a supremely regional painter – a painter of place, who took the status of the 'local artist' to new heights. Living all his life on the outskirts of Manchester, he has been celebrated as a recorder of a passing industrial vernacular, a chronicler of working-class life, a poet of the rough charm of cotton mills, alleyways, canal-side stairs, drab city churches, civic parks, the haunts of urchins and street people. That he never moved to a more cosmopolitan art centre such as London (where his work was acclaimed partly as a document of authentic northern 'otherness') has been attributed to a need to be near his familiar motifs. He certainly spoke with resignation of having 'never been abroad', as if it were one of his articles of stoic faith. At times he liked to present himself as being obsessed with the suburb of Pendlebury to the exclusion of all other ambitions in life – relationships, career, travel.

Many of Lowry's characteristic images are indeed of industrial scenes and residential streets near his home. A drawing such as *Great Ancoats Street*, Manchester (opposite) was a known, familiar haunt – a street corner that, beneath impersonal factories, might offer some homely reassurance in the mind, say, of the child loitering on the pavement in the lower left of the scene. The mood, not so different from that of certain images by Lowry's American contemporary Edward Hopper (another poet of the urban and suburban), is an uncanny, dream-like stillness, yet at the same time a documentary matter-of-factness that convinces us this is an actual place. *Oldfield Road Dwellings* (postcard 2) has another kind of truth – a dour record of the tenements' structure, a looming boat-like hulk from which the dwellers seem to trickle into the street. Here too, both the theme and the manner of the work inescapably suggest a real, rooted location. One thinks again of certain modern American painters – the Ashcan School, the Regionalists – for whom the recording of socio-topography was paramount. Lowry had periods of intensive drawing in

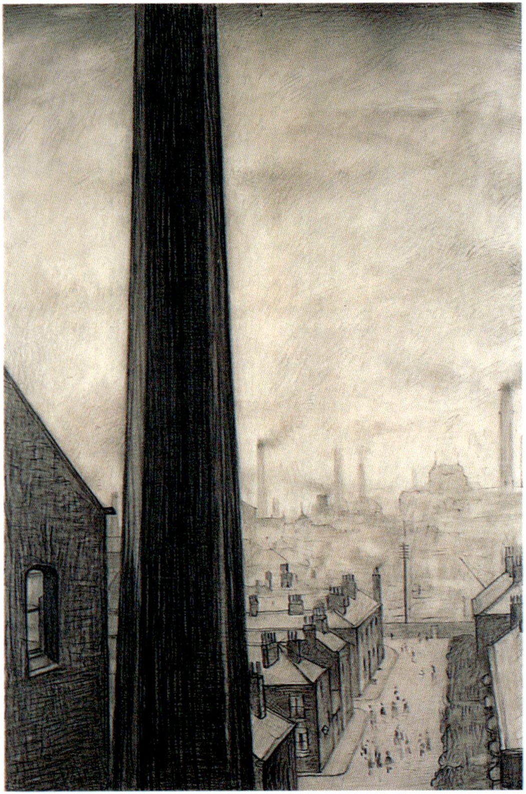

the streets (he claimed he would 'stand for hours' to observe those Dwellings for instance). He carried drawing pads for quick notational records. He also made highly finished observational works on paper such as *View from the Window of the Royal Technical College, Salford* (opposite) that testify to deep psychological investment in a view – hard looking over several sessions, married to a will towards formal resolution (note the sliver of space glimpsed between chimney and wall, narrowing to a point at the paper's bottom edge). The drawing speaks of the sharpening, again and again, of both the pencil and the observing eye. Each new detail marked in the landscape is crisply noted or softened by a rubbing finger into a relationship with the rest of the composition. Lowry, here, was studying a location special to him, from a place even more special – the high window of the college where he sought his vocation as an artist capable of giving form to perception.

Yet to make even these few observations is to begin to acknowledge that Lowry is no mere topographic recorder. He is always concerned to adapt and select from observed reality, to represent the world through the lens of his own philosophical outlook. Even in his earlier, more conventional works, *Country Lane* 1914 (page 30), or *Clifton Junction* 1910 (page 12),

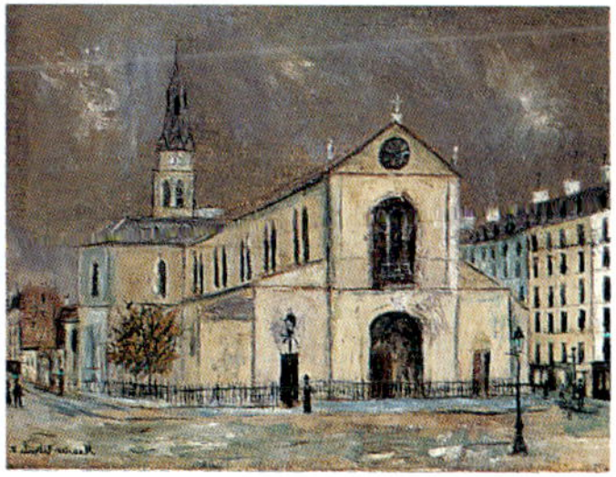

Maurice Utrillo **L'Eglise de Clignancourt c. 1915** oil

LS Lowry **Clifton Junction – Evening** **1910** oil on board

he was already in a tradition of late romantic painting (based in the nineteenth-century Hague School in Holland, in pre-impressionist French painting at Barbizon and elsewhere) which saw the 'realistic' rendition of place as anopportunity for a moody evocation of the loneliness of the human soul. Numerous major nineteenth- and twentieth-century artists – van Gogh, Mondrian – evolved through similar styles, and like those artists the young Lowry sought in landscape an expression of the human spirit. Adolph Valette, Lowry's main painting teacher, evoked a similar romantic, even symbolist atmosphere, in his delicately poetic street scenes. Lowry, in his first industrial images, softens the focus of factories into vague presences, and shows spectral passers-by, as if still seeking spiritual and lyrical qualities in the face of hard facts of life. But the melancholy of late romantic art could easily become a cliché (which van Gogh had escaped only through radical colour and rhythm, Mondrian through abstraction). Lowry's achievement in his mature work was to leave it behind in favour of much more genuinely pessimistic treatment of explicitly industrialised, unglamorised subjects. He produced a far more powerful, paradoxical sense of loneliness within the crowd, and desolation within the conurbations of human beings.

Lowry was finally to create an uncompromising statement that appears today as rigorous as much that initially seemed more radical and 'materialist' in (often abstract) 'modern art'. Giving conscious expression to the disenchantment of the twentieth century world, Lowry offers no easy hope of redemption. He could scarcely be less of a cosy chronicler of local life.

Lowry is profoundly ambivalent about the places he depicts. He described being at first repelled by the depressed district of Pendlebury when his family moved there (when he was 21), but also how he gradually became interested, finally obsessed with depicting it. The same may be said for his attitude to depicting the industrial landscape generally – that there is a repulsion

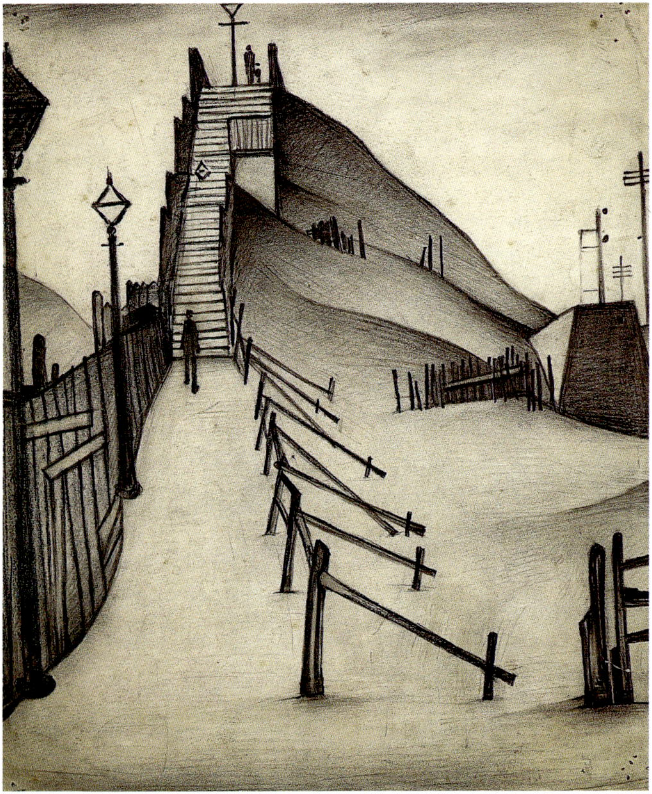

within his fascination. Far from comfortably celebrating his subject, in the grand compositions there is a suggestion of the bruised, stained and putrid in the colour. The stagnant pools and gaunt buildings are celebrated with a kind of morbidity, and the land examined as an infected body, its minute occupants infesting it like parasites. Lowry's scenes of single, stricken houses such as *House on the Moor* (postcard 5) can have a nightmarish, almost necrophiliac quality.

Lowry's frequently elevated viewpoint (recalling his Technical College window views) adds to the feeling of detached observation, and even if not literally from a high viewpoint, his tendency to stack up layers of receding hills and buildings on the picture plane creates a similar effect. Lowry is no fond poet of locality in the sense that Constable was of Dedham Vale, leading the viewer in among the farms and copses of East Anglia. Among other twentieth century British artists, there is in some ways more feeling for particular place, experienced directly through the senses, in the semi-abstractions of Peter Lanyon in Cornwall, or Ivon Hitchens in Sussex. Both give the viewer a feeling of being immersed in the particular natural light and the specific structure of their landscape. Lowry more often remains (and leaves the viewer) an outsider, looking across to some ironic travesty of a promised land. And when he does come in closer, his idea of place is often not site-specific, but quite abstract and elemental. He shows people huddling in promenade shelters, gathering around bandstands, sitting on park benches, milling around a covered street market. While these locations may have counterparts in the real world, they frequently seem to occupy an existential void. They could be anywhere.
Indeed, contrary to his stay-at-home reputation, Lowry made constant day trips and longer jaunts not only to different industrial towns (Huddersfield, Ashton-under-Lyne, Glasgow and others), but to the seaside holiday resorts (including Berwick-on-Tweed, Lytham St Anne's) that were the sociological

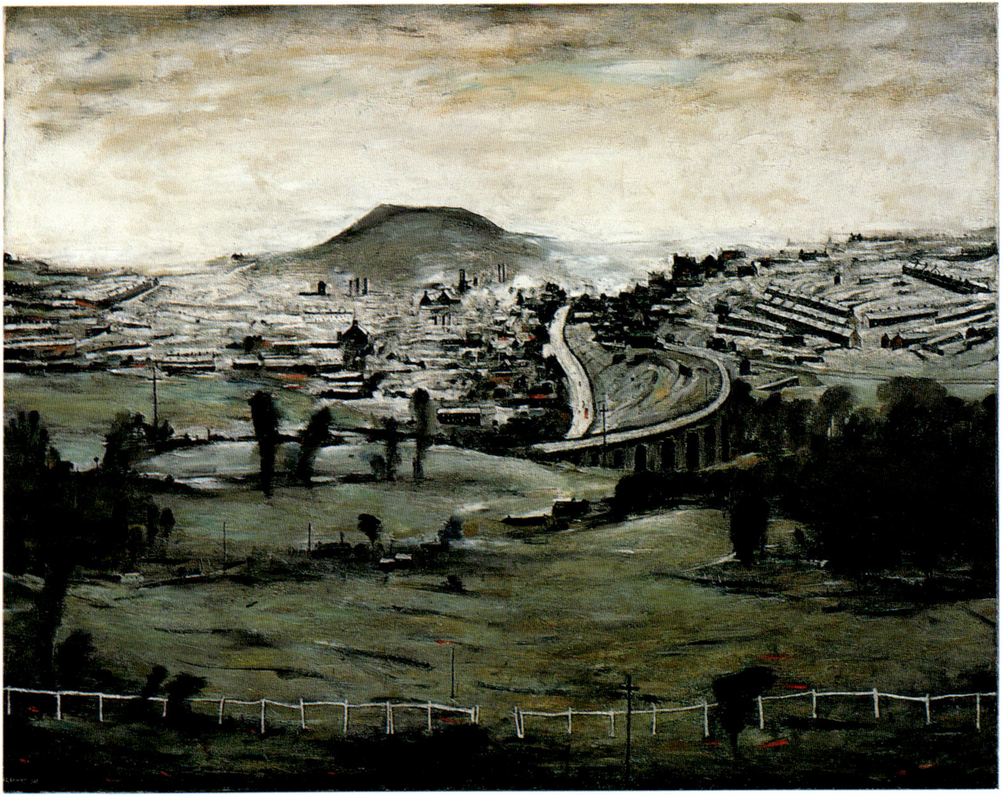

LS Lowry **Bargoed** **1965** oil on canvas

counterpart to working cities. He never ceased, alongside his city subjects, to render empty landscapes drawn from trips to the Lake District, Ireland, Wales and elsewhere, and even emptier seascapes (postcard 8). His work is usually as much about estrangement as familiarity, and more about not belonging than belonging. The role of visitor, observing the local character, suited him better than being a 'local' himself. Clearly, too, with his outsider's eye, and his tendency to merge observation with artifice, any scene might furnish elements for a painting. In fact his paintings are most often amalgams of different places, and of generic with specific features, rather than accurate depictions of specific places. His artist friend Sheila Fell remembered drawing with him in the countryside, and finding that in his sketchbook he littered the hills and dales with factories and chimneys. His paintings of empty landscape (postcard 4) indeed feature the same receding hillocks that underlie his industrial scenes, but as if seen before the arrival of industry and occupation, or after their passing. Lowry sometimes spoke of imagining a great flood engulfing human life, and his empty landscapes could almost depict the aftermath of such an event. His sea paintings – single horizons across white expanses – might also be seen as subsuming the imagery that crowds his other work: all that remains here, apart from the horizon and the faint rhythm of waves, are the softly darkened margins that so often appear at the top and bottom edge of his works like a subliminal awareness of the viewer's eyelids that could eventually close upon the scene.

Lowry's art is certainly deeply anti-naturalist. The absence of cast shadows is often remarked upon as a peculiarity and more generally there is a universal, milky light in his landscapes and city scenes that separates them from any impressionist heritage of studied light effects. Both the light and the space in his oil paintings are highly synthetic constructs. He marshals a series of pictorial conventions,

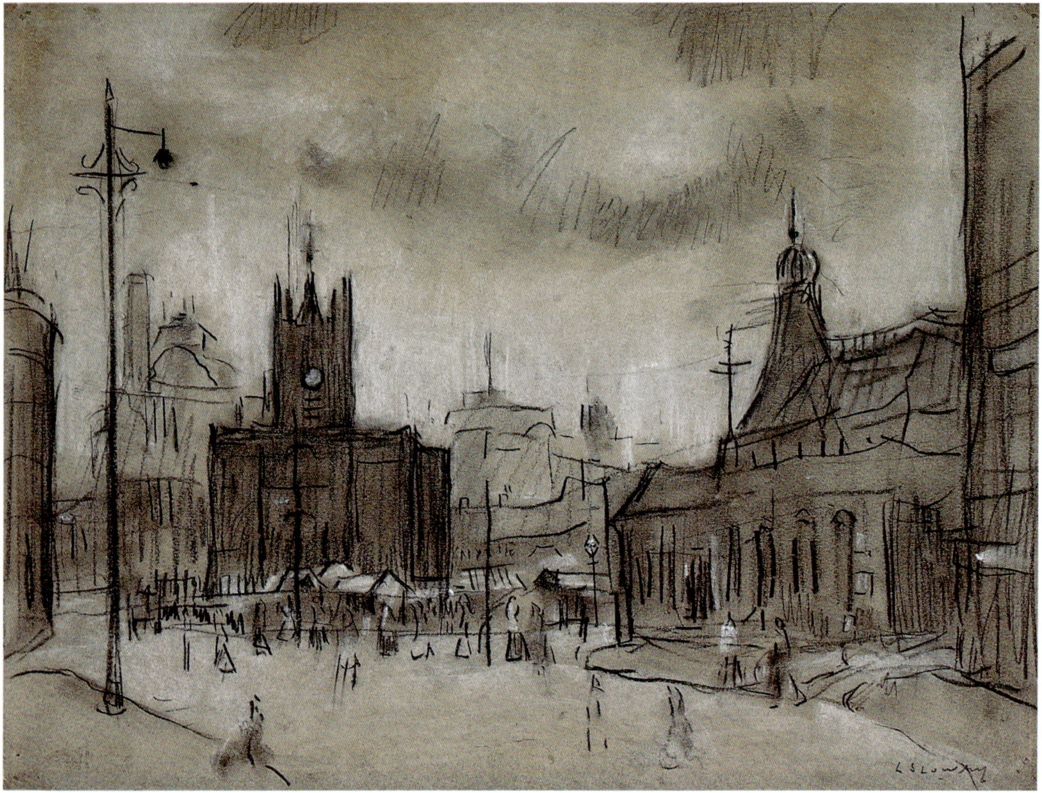

LS Lowry **The Flat Iron Market c.1925** charcoal, pencil and chalk

using a limited palette of colours worked into a thick white foundation layer, with areas of tonal gradation to suggest hills, and a mixture of overall aerial perspective and localised pockets of linear perspective in buildings, roads and canals. The effect is to conjure a mental image of the environment, with features itemised, slightly detached from each other, arranged in a way that faintly suggests an episodic, narrative sequence.

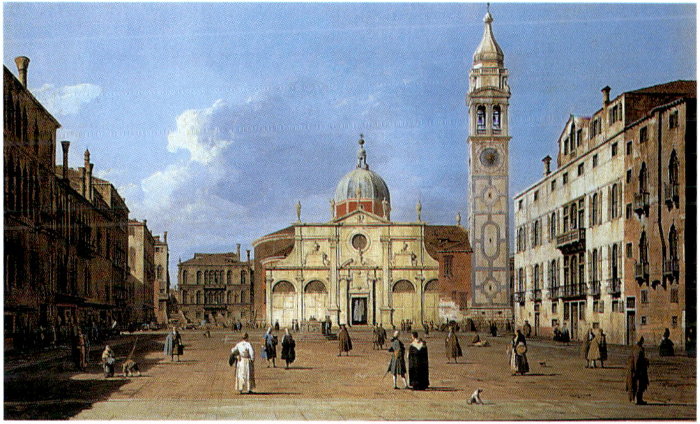

Canaletto **Campo Sta Maria Formosa c. 1731** oil

One can understand the appeal of this formula to audiences seeking a nostalgic, escapist attitude to an old fashioned work-a-day world. He can be thought to offer a quirky elegy to the town life of corner shops, workers' hob-nail boots and the grim factories that provided livelihood. His sceptical detachment from the miniaturised scenes before him can be misread as offering a toy-town quaintness. The fashion, between the wars, for naive artists

LS Lowry **The Sea** **1952** oil on canvas

in France such as Louis Vivin (who also depicted populated street scenes) and other 'Popular Realist Painters' as they were called, was often based on similar dubious sentimental attitudes to society and the 'simple life'. It is likely that the cityscapes by Lowry which were well received at the Paris Salon in the early 1930s were read in the same terms, as were Maurice Utrillo's well-known Paris scenes (page 11). Yet as we have seen – and this is true of Utrillo to some extent also – expressive and symbolic elements at work in Lowry build to a much more substantial and challenging presentation of the world.

What we have in Lowry is a modern form of the 'philosopher painters' of the seventeenth century – Poussin, with his classical temples ranged in Arcadian landscape; Ruisdael, with his dilapidated churches and mills – artists whose vision of the world embodied a whole attitude toward existence. Lowry's close affinities are generally, in fact, with pre-twentieth-century artists. It is to Canaletto's documentary views of the Venetian cityscape (page 19), peopled with passers by and decorated with processions, that we must look for antecedents to Lowry's wide-angle visions of sweeping canals and roads, and their characteristic trick of creating illusionistic box-like spaces (often a three-sided close of houses) with figures ranged in front of, or inside them. For precursors to Lowry's mountain scenes one might look to Richard Wilson's conception of landscape (this page) not as a romantic, sublime force but as a resort for human occupation, with geography seen as a quasi-mechanical structure for habitation and exploitation. Conspicuous in such enlightenment artists is an innate secularism, which was already underway in the previous century, in Dutch painting, with its demotic bustle and its token church towers subsumed as sociological features in the environment. Its roots are also in Poussin's grand landscapes and city scenes (page 25). Poussin shows us a world in which diminutive human characters conduct their lives. They process

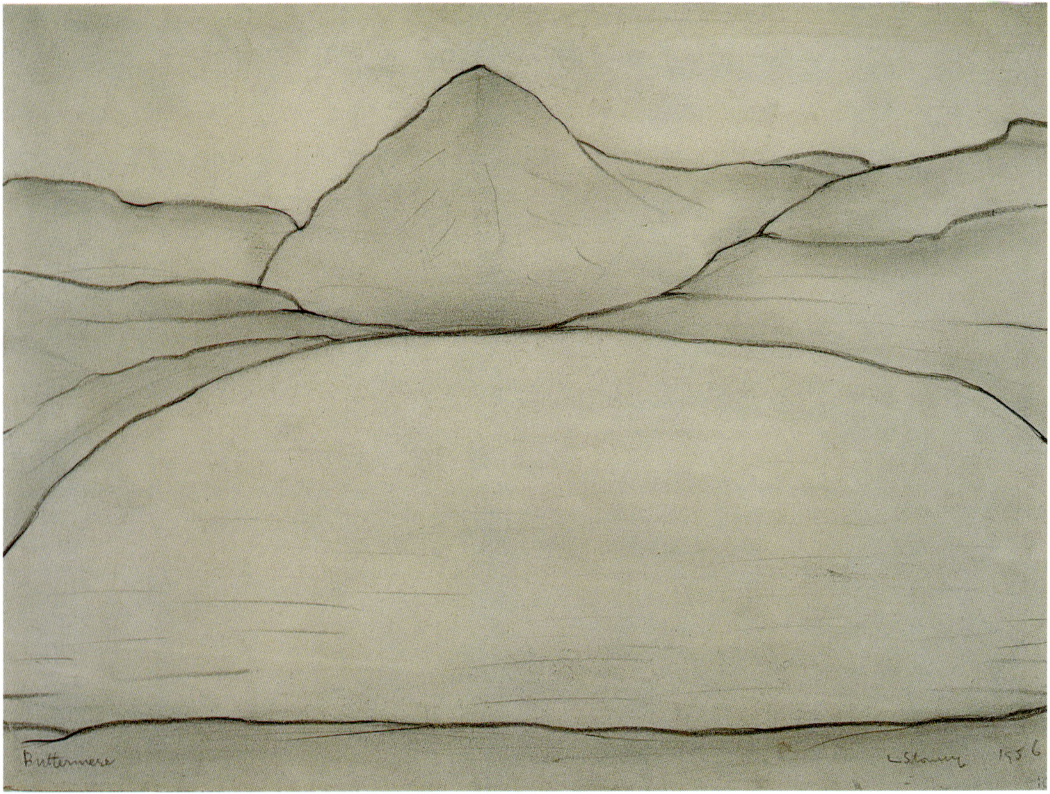
Buttermere
1956

LS Lowry **Buttermere** **1956** pencil

past temples, travel on vehicles, come into conflict, into misfortune, experience honour or dishonour, find or lose love, die and are buried. Calamities occur – flood, storm, war – and the whole is played out in front of a stage-flat space of distant receding hills, interspersed with monuments and habitations, connected by winding roads and rivers. Despite their religious subjects (Christian or pagan), the paintings convey primarily a stoical, sceptical view of human activity conducted amid the elements and within the dimensions of time and space.

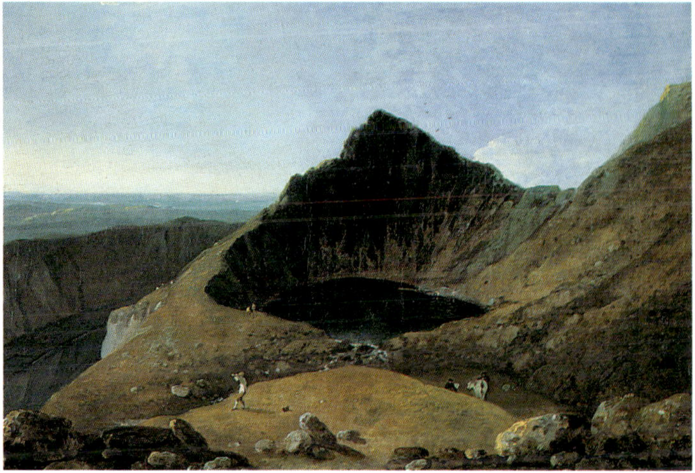

Richard Wilson **Llyn-y-Cau, Cader Idris** **exhibited 1774** oil on canvas

The action on Lowry's stage is seen in a similar spirit. Figures engage in fights, suffer accidents, go about

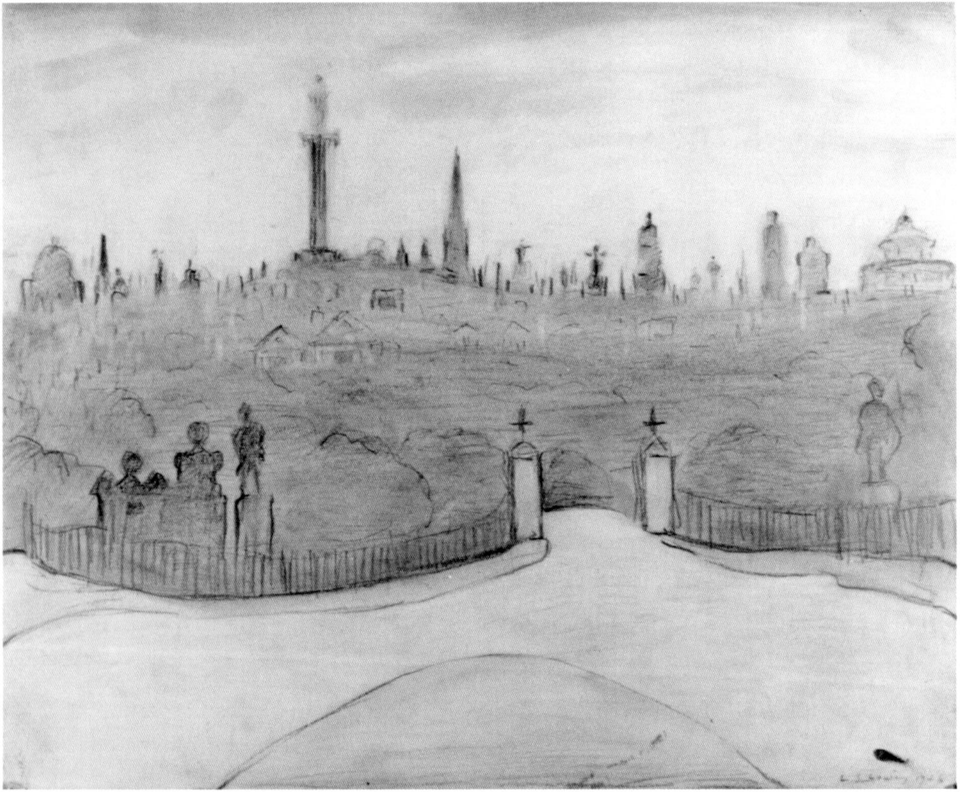

LS Lowry **The Necropolis, Glasgow** **1946** pencil

their business, are visited by fever carts, hearses, ambulances. The forces guiding human beings are not those of any supernatural power. The monolithic churches that loom in Lowry's paintings are the heavy Victorian structures of men, adrift like vessels in pictorial space, just like the factories whose chimneys alternate with steeples on the horizons. Industry is a power that will pass, as religion passed; a power that having controlled humans, will abandon them. It is human-made convention that rules the lives and actions of humans, and the buildings themselves witness the passing events through eye-like windows, impassively as Lowry did himself, before they finally become vacant and derelict.

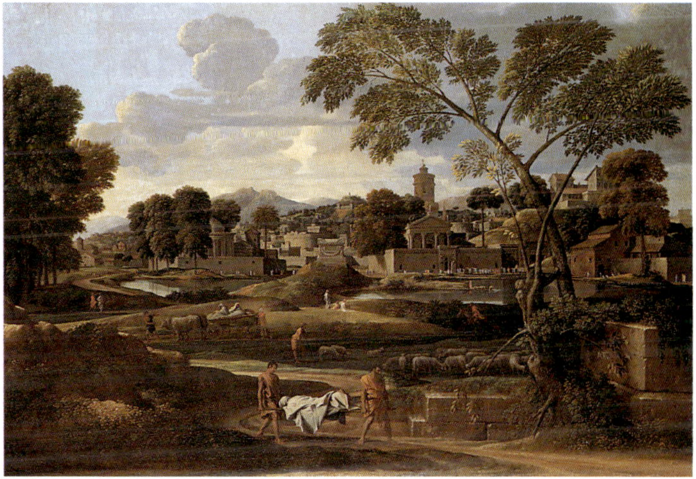

Nicholas Poussin **Landscape with the Body of Phocion carried out of Athens** **1648** oil

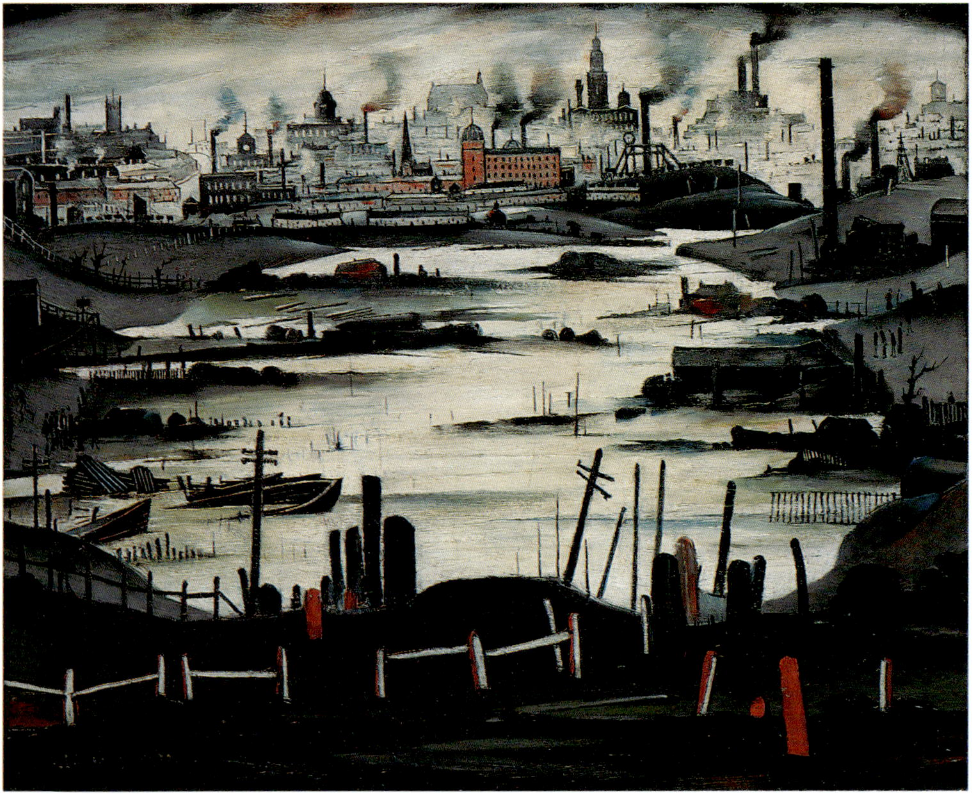

LS Lowry **The Lake** **1937** oil on canvas

His well-known picture of a man lying on a wall, cigarette echoing a smoking stack beyond, indicates the complex symbolism throughout Lowry's work. The parallels of vertical figures with lamp posts and towers, the play of vertical against horizontal, and against the diagonal drift of walking people and plumes of smoke – the whole builds to an elaborate formal diagram of the interaction of time and space, natural and man-made, activity and passivity, in which the abject and absurdist affairs of humans occur. His pictures of cemeteries (page 24) with their standing stones and statue-figures make the point again; that all cities are cities of death forming monuments to mortality.

Does Lowry offer any redemption? Does he admit any hope? He felt little optimism in his own personal life. He often dismissed his own painting activity as just another absurd pursuit, like those of the figures he painted. The mere satisfaction of having relinquished self-deception, seemed cold comfort to him. And yet, finally, there is great beauty in Lowry's pictures despite the ugliness of their subjects. There is boundless curiosity at the very unlikeliness of the world, and restlessly inventive creativity. Undoubtedly the process of painting could be therapeutic for him, releasing him from ego, taking him to 'the other side' as he said listening to music did. In his work there are, finally, the elements of celebration, even serenity, even splendour. What is so heroic – paradoxically adding to the splendour of his achievement – is that he achieves the affirmation he does without compromising his realism. He made painting itself a place of refuge without softening its representation of all he sought refuge from.

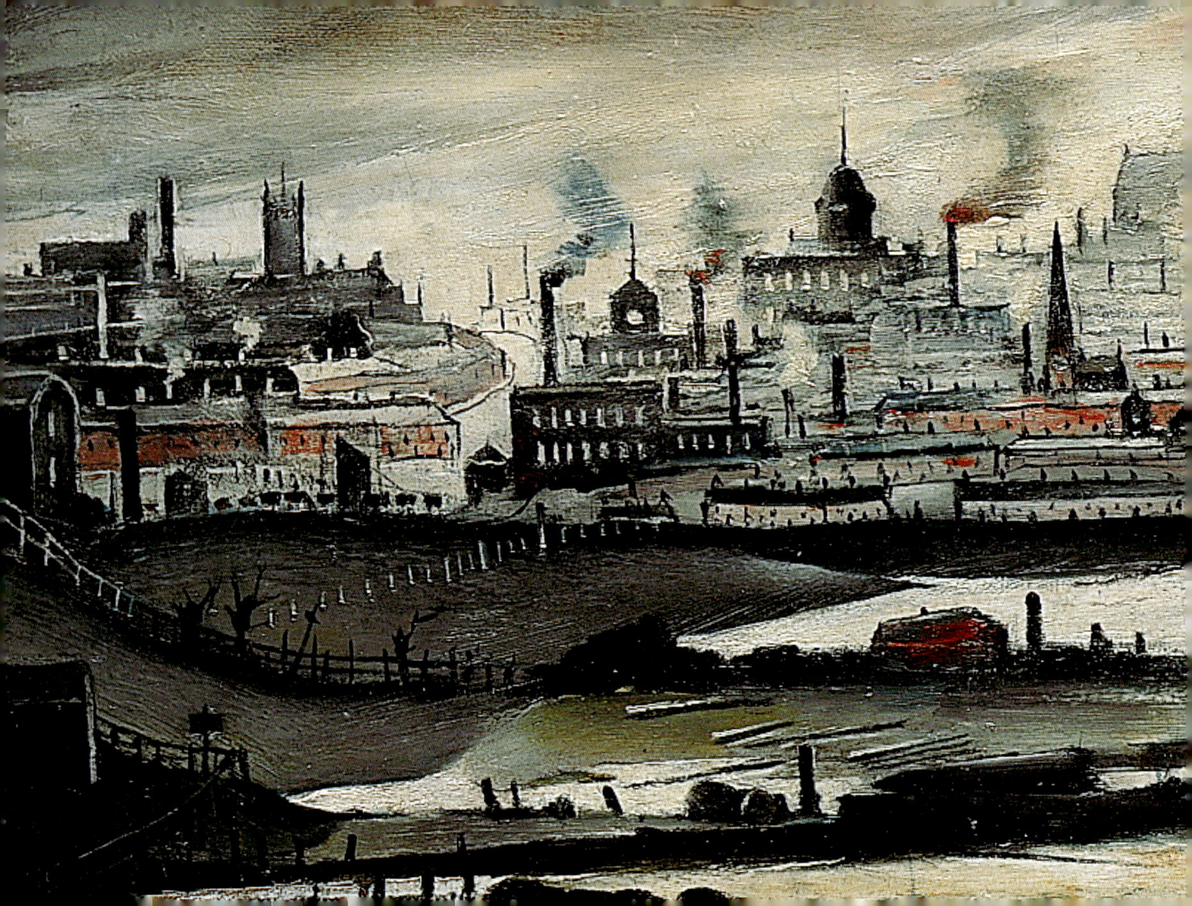

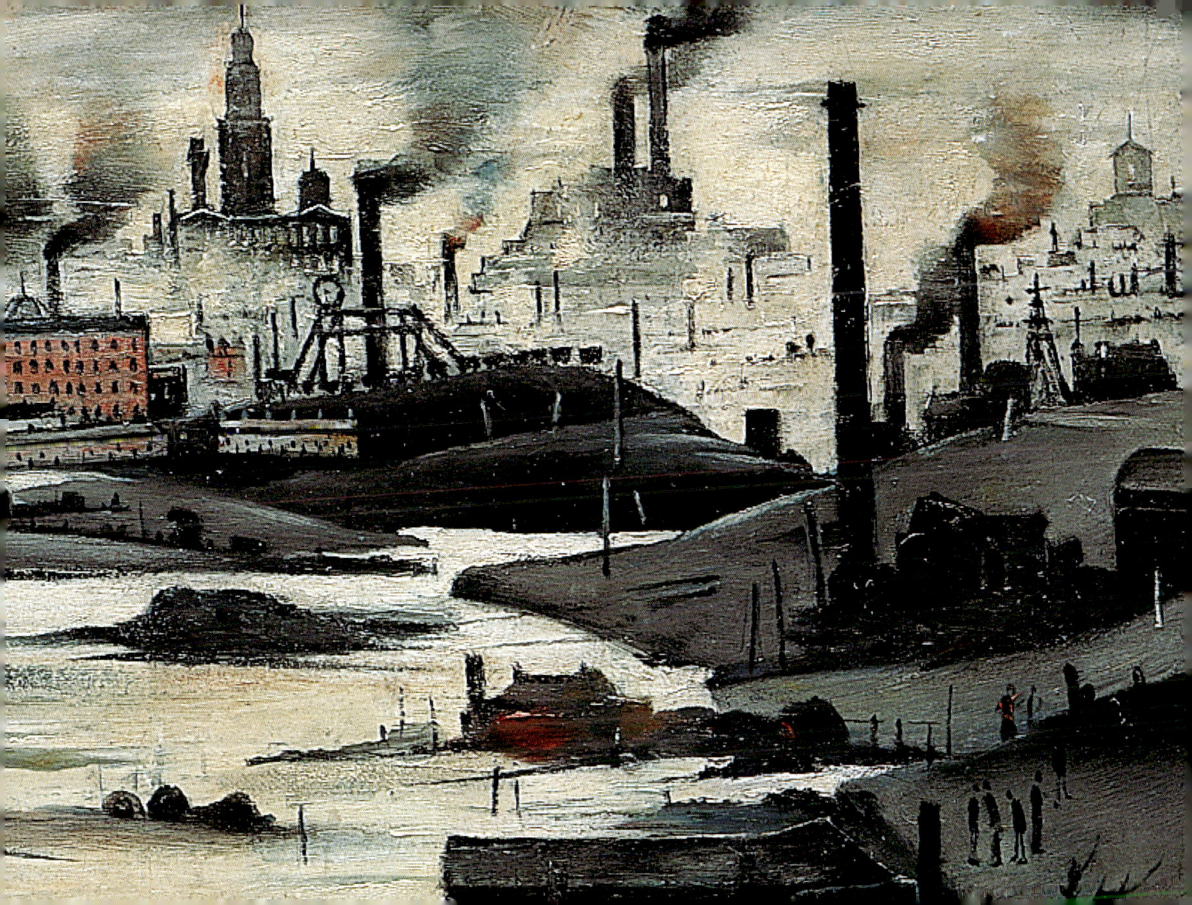

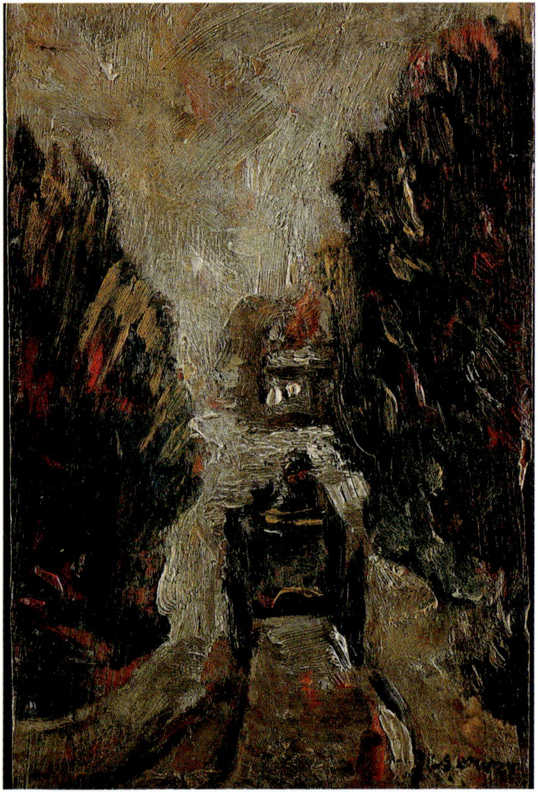

List of Works Exhibited

Lowry Collection, Salford:

Industrial Landscape
1953/57, oil

Coming from the Mill
1930, oil

Pendlebury Scene
1931, pencil

Dean's Mill, Swinton
c.1946 pencil

The Lake
1937, oil

The River Irwell at the Adelphi
1924, pencil

Bargoed
1965, oil

Mill Scene
1965, oil

A Street Scene (St Simon's Church)
1927, pencil

The Flat Iron Market
c.1925, pencil, charcoal and white chalk

A View from the window of the Royal Technical College, Salford
1924, pencil

Newtown Mill & Bowling Green
c.1928, pencil

The Sea,
1963, oil

Seascape
1952, oil

Yachts
1920, pastel

Yachts
1959, watercolour

The Estuary
1956, watercolour

Waiting for the Tide, South Shields
1967, oil

Boats
1956, pencil

On the Thames
c.1965, pencil

A Ship
c.1965, oil

Clifton Junction – Morning
1910, oil

Clifton Junction – Evening
1910, oil

A Fylde Farm
1918, crayon and pencil

Country Lane
1914, oil

Regent Street, Lytham
1922, oil

Swinton Moss
1922, oil

On the Moss
1923, pencil

Country Road
1925, pencil

Country Road near Lytham
1925, pencil

Lancashire Landscape
1913, pastel

Landscape in Cumberland
1951, oil

House on the Moor
1950, oil

The Lake
1951, oil

A Landmark
1936, oil

Glencoe
1956, pencil

12 Pins, Cumbria
c.1955, pencil

Buttermere
1956, pencil

Houses on a Hill
1960, pencil

By the County Court, Salford
1926, pencil

By Christ Church, Salford
1926, pencil

Great Ancoats Street, Manchester
1930, pencil

Behind Leaf Square (1)
1926, pencil

An Old Lamp: Behind Leaf Square (4)
1926, pencil

Francis Terrace, Salford
1956, pencil

The Necropolis, Glasgow
1946, pencil

Man in an Archway
c.1965, pencil

Chimney
c.1965, pencil

St Augustine's Church, Pendlebury
1930, pencil

Christ Church, Salford
1956, pencil

Church in Hulme
c.1957, pencil

Oldfield Road Dwellings
1929, pencil

Worsley (Iron Bridge)
1925, pencil

Canal at Worsley
1925, pencil

Bridge with figures over Colliery Railway,
undated, pencil

Tin Mine near Gunnard's Head
1955, pencil

Ancoats
1967, pencil

Maryport
c.1968, pencil

People on the Sands
c.1920, pencil

In Edinburgh
c.1960, pencil

The Post Office
1926, pencil

Private collections:

Stockport Viaduct
1944, oil

Industrial Scene
1951, oil

Beach Scene, Lytham
1963, oil

An Ancient Path
1931, pencil

Ship entering Princess Dock, Glasgow
1947, oil

Queens Dock, Glasgow
1947, oil

Spittal Sands, Berwick
1960, oil

Rhuddlan Castle
1924, pencil

Crowther Street, Stockport
1934, pencil

Mill Yard, Tottington, near Bury
1921, pencil

Stormy Sea
1968, oil

Waiting for the Tide
1965, oil

Stormy Sea
1968, oil

Pastoral, Lytham Farm
1920, pastel

A Fylde Farm
1945, oil on panel

Steps in Oldham
1970, pencil

The Corner Shop
1970, pencil

Hill Farm in the Peak District
1936, pencil

Blackpool Tower
1923, pencil

Glencoe
1959, oil on panel

Mountain in Ireland
undated, pencil

Sea at Sunderland
1965, oil on panel

Going to the Match
1953, oil
The Professional Footballers Association

Early Morning
1954, oil
The Cryne/ Graham collection

Canal Scene near Accrington
1939, oil
The Cryne/ Graham collection

Albion Mill
1941, oil
The Cryne/ Graham collection

Seascape
1944, pencil

Arden's Farm, Swinton
1930, pencil

After the Blitz
1942, oil

Mill Scene
1959, oil
Glossopdale Community College Association (PTA)

Coronation Street
1957, oil

Steps
undated, pencil

Tower at Waterford
1965, pencil

Public collections:

Huddersfield
1965, oil
Huddersfield Art Gallery

View from Chapel Hill, Huddersfield
1965, pencil
Huddersfield Art Gallery

Industrial Panorama
1953, oil
Nottingham Castle Museum

Our Town
1943, oil
Rochdale Art Gallery

Ebbw Vale
1960, oil
The Herbert Art Gallery & Museum

Greenwich Reach towards Deptford Power Station
1959, oil
The National Maritime Museum, Greenwich

River Wear at Sunderland
1961, oil
Sunderland Museum & Art Gallery (Tyne & Wear Museums)

A Street in Stockport: Crowther Street
1930, oil
Stockport Art Gallery

Thanks to staff at all the galleries and to the private collectors who have generously loaned works for **Lowry's Places**. We would like especially to thank Peggy Finlayson and Carol Ann Lowry.

Lowry's Places exhibition 16 September 2000 – 3 January 2001 curated by Lindsay Brooks.

Publishing and editorial direction: Roger Sears
Art Direction: David Pocknell and Martin Tilley
Designed by Martin Tilley at Pocknell Studio

Published by the Lowry Press
The Lowry
Pier 8 Salford Quays M5 2AZ
Telephone: 44 (0)i61 876 2104
Fax: 44 (0)161 876 2021
www.thelowry.com
First published 2000

A CIP catalogue record of this book is available from The British Library
ISBN 1 902970 08 X
Originated, printed and bound in the UK by Colt Press

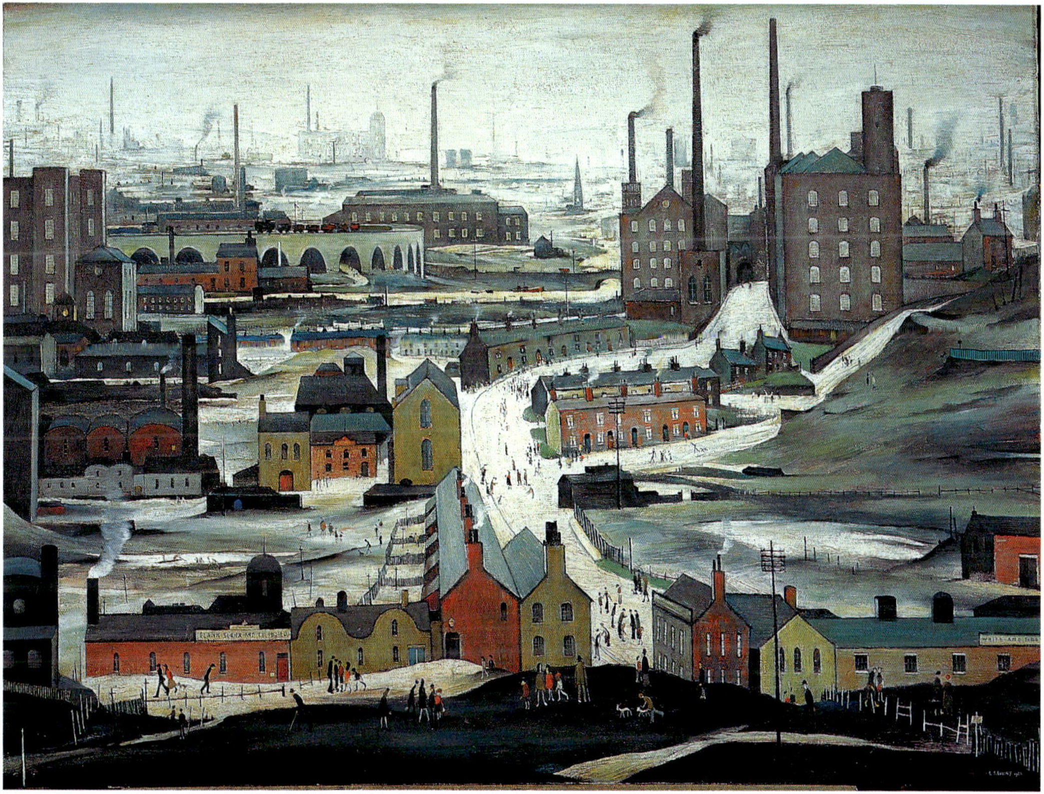

LS Lowry **Industrial Scene, Ashton-under-Lyne** **1952** oil on canvas

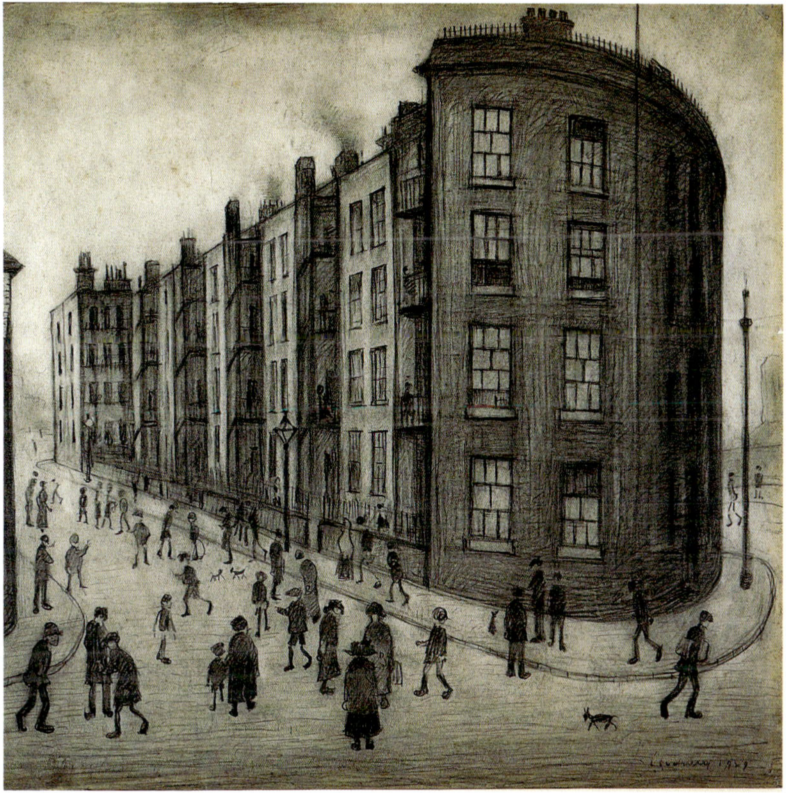

LS Lowry Oldfield Road Dwellings 1927 pencil

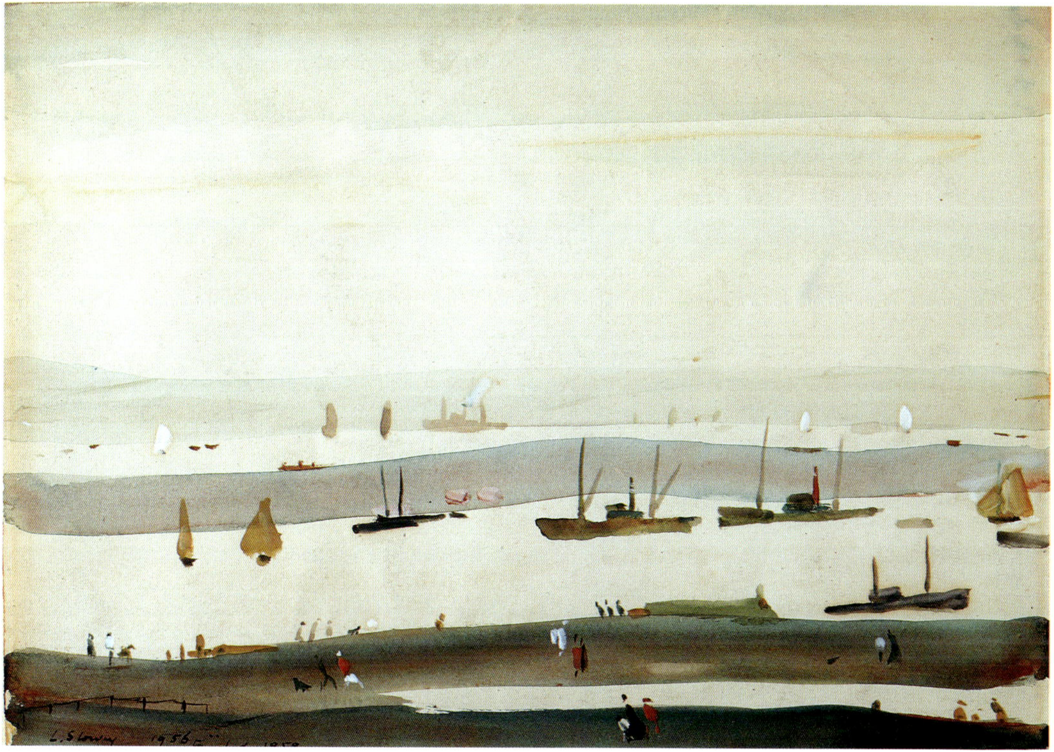
L.S. Lowry 1956

LS Lowry **The Estuary** **1956–9** watercolour

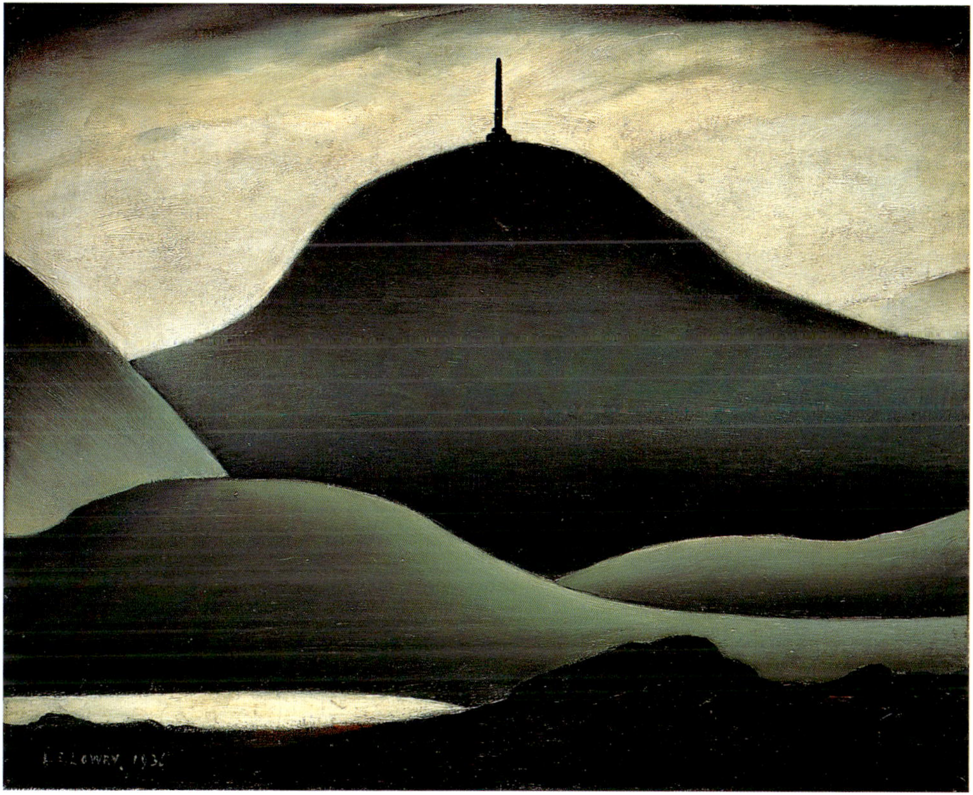
LOWRY

LS Lowry **A Landmark** **1936** oil on canvas

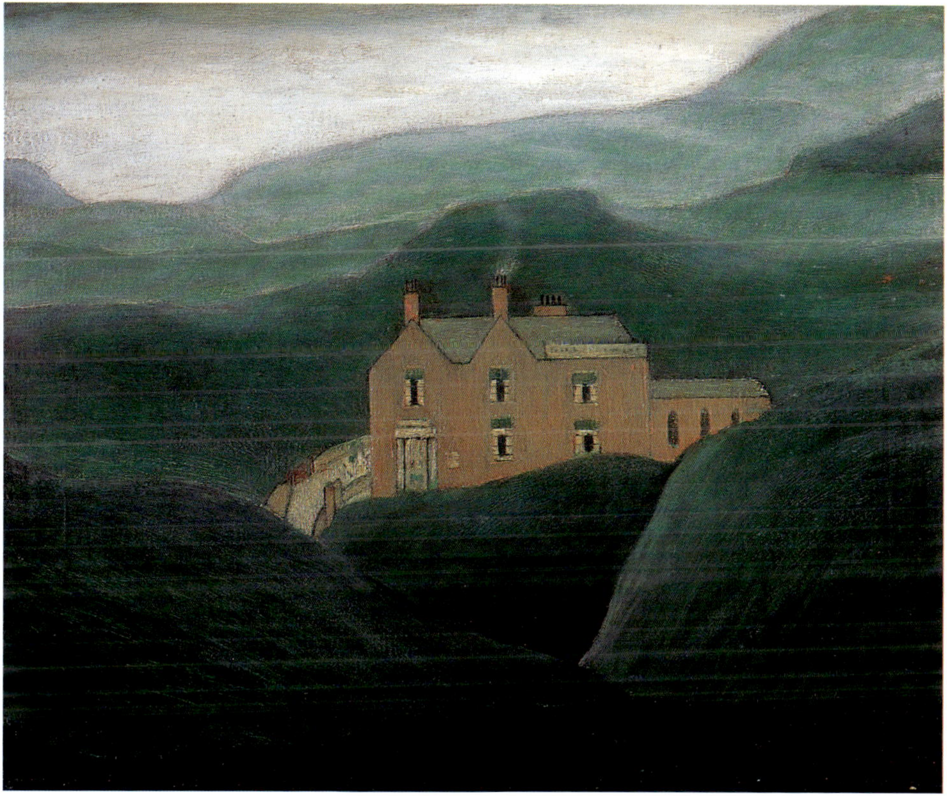

LS Lowry **House on the Moor** **1950** oil on canvas

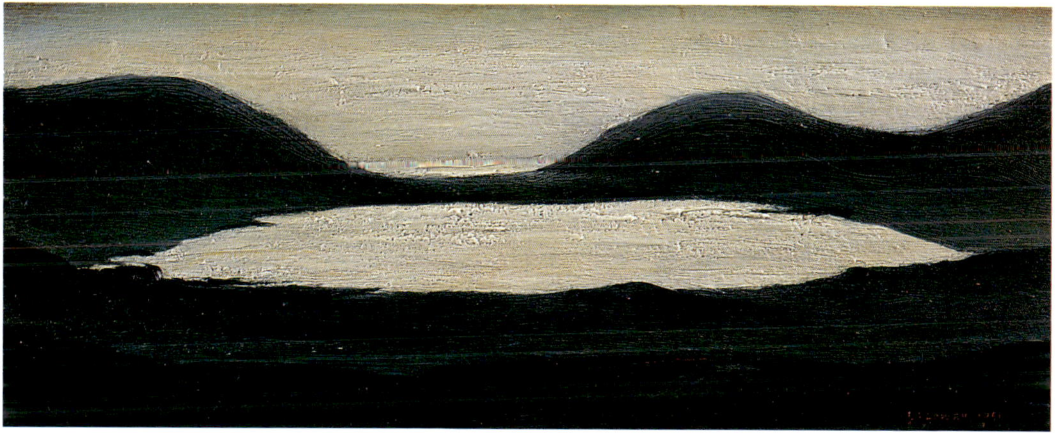

LS Lowry **The Lake** **1951** oil on board

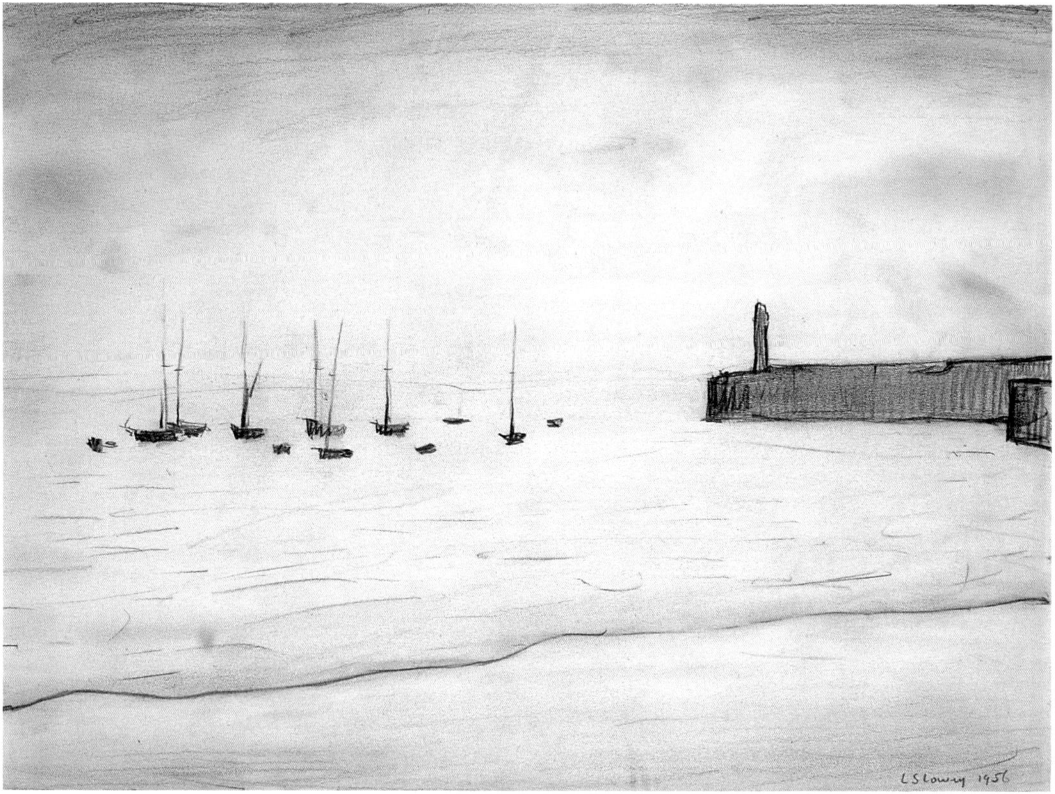
LSLowry 1956

LS Lowry **Boats** **1956** pencil

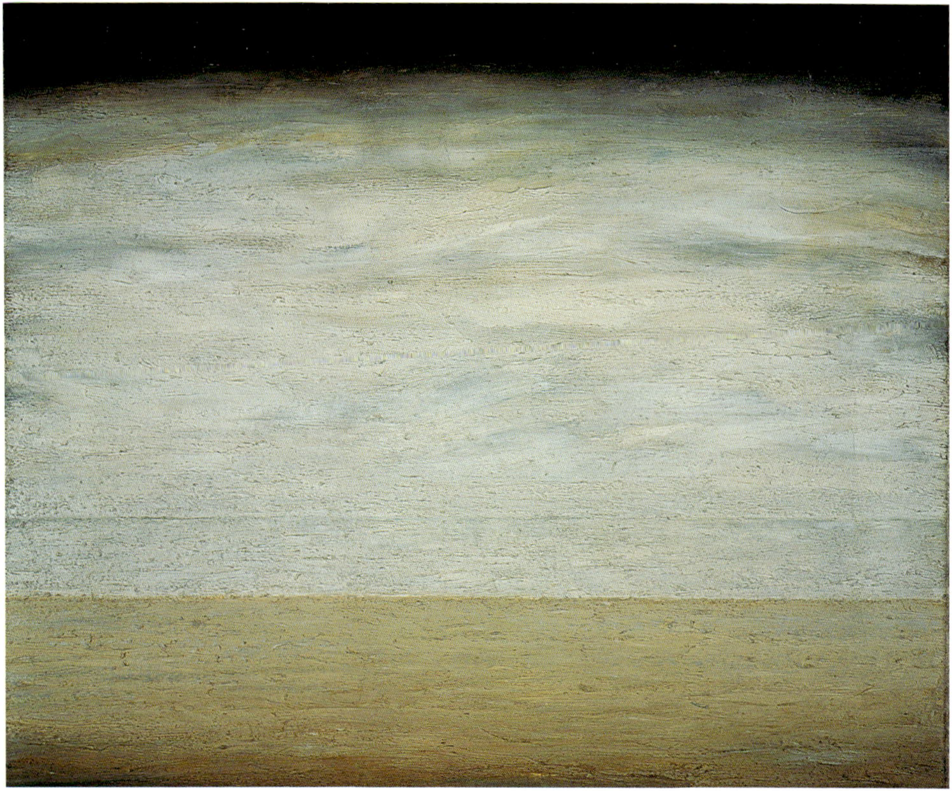

LS Lowry **Seascape** **1952** oil on canvas